FAMILY LIFE IN
Saxon Britain

PETER HICKS

Wayland

FAMILY LIFE SERIES:

Medieval Britain

Roman Britain

Saxon Britain

Second World War

Tudors & Stuarts

Victorian Britain

Series design: Pardoe Blacker Ltd
Editors: Sarah Doughty and Katie Orchard
Production Controller: Carol Stevens

First published in 1994 by Wayland (Publishers) Ltd
61 Western Road, Hove, East Sussex BN3 1JD, England

© Copyright 1994 Wayland (Publishers) Ltd

British Library Cataloguing in Publication Data
Hicks, Peter
 Family Life in Saxon Britain. – (Family Life Series)
  I.Title II.Series
  306.850941

ISBN 0 7502 1220 9

Printed and bound in Italy by Rotolito Lombarda S.p.A.

Cover pictures: A bustling Saxon village, a Saxon pot with runic symbols and a Saxon buckle.

Picture acknowledgements: The Bodleian Library, Oxford 18 (top); the Bridgeman Art Library 10, 11 (top and bottom), 12 (bottom), 13 (top and bottom), 21 (bottom), 28 (top); C M Dixon *cover* 20; Mark Gardiner 26; Peter Hicks 5, 6 (top), 7 (top), 16 (top), 19 (bottom), 24; Michael Holford 8 (bottom), 9 (top); the Mansell Collection 22 (bottom); Southampton City Heritage 15 (top); York Archaeological Trust 18 (bottom), 19 (top), 21 (top), 22 (top), 25 (top, middle and bottom), 27 (top and bottom), 28 (bottom), 29 (top and bottom). Artwork: Peter Dennis *cover* 4 (bottom), 5, 6 and 7 (bottom), 14, 17, 23; Peter Bull 4 (top), 8 (top), 15 (bottom), 16 (bottom). The remaining pictures are from the Wayland Picture Library.

CONTENTS

THE SAXONS ARRIVE

The people of Britain were conquered by the Romans in AD 43. The Romans built towns and roads and brought to Britain their own language and **culture**. Britons lived under Roman rule for almost 400 years. In AD 407, after the collapse of the **Roman Empire**, the Romans finally left Britain. Before they went, they warned the Britons that the country was now open for the Anglo-Saxons to invade.

It is often imagined that the Anglo-Saxons were warlike invaders. This idea came from the writings of historians Gildas (in the sixth century), and **Bede** (in the eighth century). Archaeologists now think that the arrival of the Anglo-Saxons was a lot more peaceful. There was violence – some of the Roman-British people tried to defend their land, and the battles went on until 600 AD. But generally the Anglo-Saxons settled and mixed in surprisingly quickly.

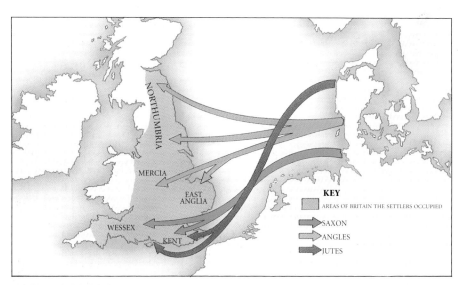

KEY

AREAS OF BRITAIN THE SETTLERS OCCUPIED

SAXON

ANGLES

JUTES

This map shows the possible routes of the Angle, Saxon and Jute migrations to Britain in the fifth century.

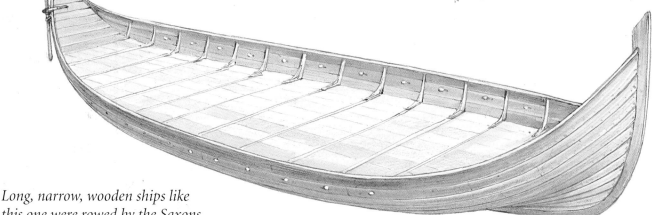

Long, narrow, wooden ships like this one were rowed by the Saxons across the North Sea, each carrying up to fifty men.

THE JOURNEY

The Saxons were a northern people coming from what we now call Germany. The Angles came from Denmark. The Angles, Saxons (from which we get the name 'Anglo-Saxon') and Jutes were all invaders. They crossed the North Sea in their open ships looking for places to settle in England. Because the sea is often cold and rough this journey must have been very dangerous. The ships probably kept to the safety of the coast before crossing at the shortest point towards England. When they reached the coast they searched for rivers to sail up and explore for good land. The Anglo-Saxons were farmers and were very keen to discover green and **fertile** valleys to **cultivate**.

*Pevensey, one of the forts built by the Romans late in the third century to counter Saxon raiders looking for rich pickings in south-east Britain. It was the scene of a terrible **massacre** of its British defenders by the Saxons in AD 491.*

WHY THE ANGLO-SAXONS CAME

We are not sure why the Anglo-Saxons came to Britain; they may have been looking for new land. Their population was increasing, but at the same time people from Asia were arriving and settling in their countries in northern Europe. Land was becoming scarce, especially as coastal areas of the region were becoming flooded because of a rise in the level of the North Sea. Many people decided to risk everything and make the dangerous sea crossing to England.

SAXON VILLAGERS

The first arrivals took the most land and built their settlements in fertile river valleys. Others who came later had to make do with less fertile land, usually on higher ground. In this uncertain world the family – which included all blood relatives – was very important. The Anglo-Saxons called this '**kinship**', a grouping of relatives that gave them greater security.

(Left) Part of the reconstructed Anglo-Saxon village of West Stow, Suffolk. The village would have probably housed four or five families. The huts were usually built in groups, and each group belonged to one family.

AN ANGLO-SAXON VILLAGE

At West Stow, a village in Suffolk, we can find out what an early settlement was like. The layout of the village has been preserved in a deposit of sand so we can find clues as to how it looked. By studying the foundations, seventy different types of buildings that were lived in through the period AD 400 to 600 have been found. By reconstructing some of the buildings we can see what life could have been like for an Anglo-Saxon 'ceorl' (farm worker) and his family.

The village was made up of a group of farms, enclosed by a ditch and fence. This was usually to keep young children and livestock in and wild animals out.

The hall would have been an important place for the families in the village who would meet in the hall and sleep in the huts.

In each group of buildings there were single-roomed buildings for sleeping and workshops or store houses, centred around a hall.

The main building was the hall, probably a **communal** building, surrounded by smaller huts. Most of the huts at West Stow were quite spacious, with a high beam from which hung a **cauldron**. It is easy to imagine the family huddling around it exchanging poems and stories to entertain themselves during the long, cold winter nights.

Some of the houses at Stow had sunken floors with planks built over them. It seems that many of these houses were used as workshops with storage space underneath. The post holes in the ground tell us that the houses had upright structures to hold up the roof. The walls were made of split wooden planks. The whole family would have helped to build these houses, from cutting the trees to **thatching** the roof.

BRITAIN IN SAXON TIMES

Jarlshof

SCOTLAND

Lindisfarne

NORTHUMBRIA

IRELAND

MERCIA

WALES

EAST ANGLIA

CORNWALL   WESSEX   KENT

Saxon Britain was divided into kingdoms ruled by kings. Kent was the first kingdom to become rich and powerful, followed by East Anglia and Northumbria.

RICH FAMILIES

Some of the settlers had very different lives to the hardworking village farmers of Stow. By AD 600, the Anglo-Saxons had developed four powerful kingdoms: Northumbria in the north; Mercia in the midlands; East Anglia to the east; and Wessex to the south. The kingdoms were ruled by royal families who were very wealthy. We can see how wealthy families were from the discovery of treasures found at Sutton Hoo.

SUTTON HOO

At Sutton Hoo lay the treasures and weapons of a very wealthy king (although his body was never found). This is some of the finest treasure ever found in Europe. The burial chamber was full of riches. See the gold and garnet purse lid below, which contained thirty-seven coins and three blanks. It is believed that these were payment for the forty oarsmen taking the dead king to the next world. We can tell the king was a warrior. His helmet was found, along with a man's sword, shield, mail coat and spears. The king's skeleton has not survived. Some think the burial was that of King Redwald, an important East Anglian king who died in AD 625.

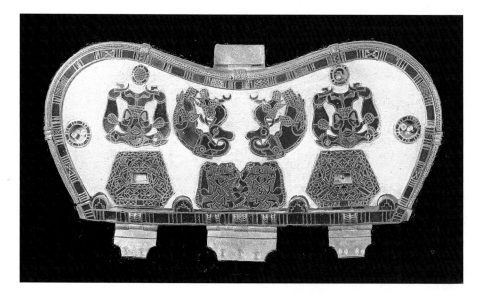

The gold and garnet purse belonging to the king originally contained a leather pouch for the coins, but the actual pouch has rotted away.

HOMES

We can also find out about the homes rich families would have lived in. More than seven royal palaces have been found. One of the best was found at Yeavering in Northumbria. This shows a hall and a number of different types of buildings. The great Anglo-Saxon poem *Beowulf* tells us that in these halls, kings and their warriors had huge feasts, with food, drink, singing and story-telling. Until the Yeavering discovery, it was thought the poet had exaggerated. But this, with the Sutton Hoo finds – drinking horns and lyres – suggests *Beowulf* is accurate.

This picture shows the Sutton Hoo helmet belonging to the king. It was put together from pieces found in the soil. When it was complete, it would have had a fine carved decoration.

A golden shoulder clasp (right) and a disc brooch (left) found at Sutton Hoo.

FARMING AND FOOD

Most people in Anglo-Saxon Britain were farmers. Daily life was a constant battle to provide food for the family. Failure to provide food meant shortages and possible starvation. Farmers grew crops, reared animals, caught fish in nearby rivers and streams and probably hunted wild animals.

Hewing (cutting) wood. Wood was used for buildings, fences and repairs. Wood rots so it would have constantly needed replacing.

SUBSISTENCE FARMING

The early Anglo-Saxons were **subsistence** farmers – they produced only the food they needed for themselves. We know that the farmers kept animals. Sheep provided meat, milk and wool. Pigs, goats and cows were kept as well. Oxen were used for dragging, ploughing, and pulling heavy timber and carts. Cows – much smaller than they are today – were kept for milk and meat. Their horns were cut off, perhaps to use as drinking vessels or as raw material for tools and weapons. Barley, rye and wheat were the main crops grown. Every so often, extra food was grown and sold to buy luxury goods such as jewellery and glass. These objects must have brightened up a very hard life.

Shepherds with their flock. Anglo-Saxons made their clothes by spinning wool from sheep.

THE FARMING YEAR

The working year was very tough in the small enclosed fields around the village. In the spring, men ploughed fields, sowed seeds by hand and cleared ditches. In the summer, the most important jobs were shearing the sheep, weeding and fertilizing the soil. Weeding was a dull task perhaps carried out by children. The Anglo-Saxon name for July was 'Weodmonath' – the month of weeds!

Reaping the harvest. Harvesting was the most important task of the year.

In autumn, the harvest took place. All the family had jobs to do, from reaping the corn and tying it into sheaves, to storing the grain. Repairs to houses and thatched roofs had to be done before the winter. As there was never enough hay to feed all the animals during the winter, some animals were killed for food. This happened in October – known as 'Blotmonath' – the blood month! The meat was then salted or smoked to preserve it for the months to come.

(Above) It was important to get the year's harvest in quickly, for sudden rainstorms could destroy it and cause food shortages during the winter.

Despite the freezing temperatures of winter, work still went on. **Threshing** took place – men would hit the ears of wheat with sticks to separate the grain. The grain was then ground into flour. Timber would be cut and split for the next year's building and the orchards were pruned.

Winnowing and threshing. These tasks separated the grain from the chaff. This was winter work and people found it dull and tiring.

THE GROWTH OF TOWNS

A great change to life in the country came with the growth of towns. With so many new towns with hungry populations, farmers had to produce more food. This was good for farmers and their families because they could make money selling their produce at the market.

Large wagons like these were used to take market produce to town.

By the tenth century, farmers were providing a huge variety of food. So many cattle, pigs, sheep and goats were reared that they were taken 'on the hoof' into town, where they were killed.

There was a good choice of vegetables to buy such as carrots, parsnips, celery and cabbage. Fruits such as apples, sloes, bilberries, blackberries and raspberries were grown. Dairy produce like milk, butter and cheese was probably also available. Families in the countryside became richer because they could sell their goods at the market. These new markets brought them prosperity. They could buy the same goods that were sold in the towns. Life for farmers was slowly getting better.

Exhausting work in the fields. The men are breaking and turning the soil and sowing and raking the grass.

TOWN LIFE

For hundreds of years after the Romans left Britain, no towns or cities were built. The Anglo-Saxon settlers were not town dwellers, preferring to live in their scattered villages. The magnificent Roman towns and cities crumbled away. However, by the seventh and eighth centuries, the rich regional kings founded a series of 'wics', or towns.

THE ARRIVAL OF THE DANES

These settlements lay by the coast or rivers and were important for trade in luxury goods. Hamwic (Southampton) Gipeswic (Ipswich) and Ludenwic (London) were busy ports visited by ships from all over Europe. It seems that the ordinary people of Hamwic were involved in craft production, especially metalwork. Ludenwic was a very busy port at this time. The historian Bede, in AD 731-2 called it 'an emporium [trading centre] of many people coming by land and sea'. However these early towns did not survive because of Viking raids in the eighth and ninth centuries. Some of the Vikings were Danes – their armies were searching for parts of England to conquer. People all over eastern and southern England were terrified of the Vikings.

In late Anglo-Saxon towns, timbered houses were built. They were usually constructed over cellars dug under ground in the gravelled streets.

BURGHS

King Alfred became king of Wessex in AD 870 and responded by building a series of towns called 'burghs'. In Anglo-Saxon 'burgh' means fort. King Alfred wanted to protect his people from attack, but he also wanted to increase trade and wealth, so many burghs became excellent centres of **commerce**. This happened in neighbouring Mercia as well.

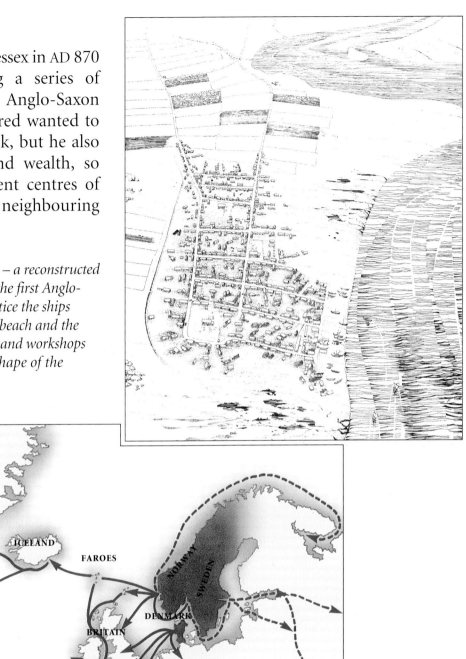

(Right) Hamwic – a reconstructed picture of one of the first Anglo-Saxon towns. Notice the ships drawn up on the beach and the groups of houses and workshops within the grid shape of the streets.

KEY

Viking Homeland

- - -> Trade routes

——> Trade and settlement

GREENLAND

ICELAND

FAROES

NORWAY

SWEDEN

DENMARK

BRITAIN

ATLANTIC OCEAN

FRANCE

NEWFOUNDLAND

MEDITERRANEAN SEA

AFRICA

The Vikings came from Scandinavia and many of them settled in northern and eastern Britain from the eighth to the eleventh century.

The high walls of the burgh at Wareham, Dorset. You can still walk round the three sides of the town on the walls today. The town was protected on the south side by the River Frome.

A typical burgh had high walls for protection. Some were stone, but many were made of earth and **turf**. If you look at the walls at Wareham in Dorset, today you will see that they are still quite high. In Alfred's time they would have been much taller, with a timber fence crowning the top. The gates would have been protected and at night they would have been locked. Inside the walls was a grid of streets which contained houses, workshops, churches, shops, inns, markets and rubbish and sewage pits. Most of these burghs were a great success and they were crowded, busy and fairly safe places for families to live and work.

*After Alfred defeated the Danes in AD 878 they were confined to an area known as **Danelaw**.*

KEY

The Danelaw

Saxon Kingdoms

THE DIVISION BETWEEN THE SAXONS AND THE DANES

NORTHUMBRIA

MERCIA

EAST ANGLIA

WESSEX

Town life in Jorvik. York was captured by the Danes in AD 867 and it became one of the biggest towns in the world with about 2,000 houses. This is a cut-away picture of a typical house, showing the inside and outside.

JORVIK

The areas settled by the Danes were eventually called **Danelaw.** The city of York (Jorvik) perhaps gives us the best idea what everyday town life was like in the late Anglo-Saxon period. Coppergate was a part of Jorvik where craftsmen and their families lived. They had **timber-post houses** with **wattle and daub** walls and thatched roofs. The houses must have been crowded because some had workshops at the back and stalls at the front where they sold their products. Each house had one room with a large square hearth. Everyone ate, slept, prayed, cooked, spun, weaved, chatted and argued in the same room. A lot of objects must have been fastened to the walls and rafters to make as much space on the floor as possible.

LIVELIHOOD

The type of work that went on in Jorvik was varied. Clearly iron-working was important. The **smithies** made tools, weapons, dress-fittings (tin-plated) and knives of very high quality. Beads, pendants and rings made of jet and amber have been found – evidence of the thriving jewellery trade. Glass-workers made and sold their wares, whilst craftwork in leather, bone, antler and wood was widespread. In fact, **wood turning** was a speciality in Coppergate and high-quality bowls and spoons survived in the damp conditions for over a thousand years! The wood-workers would have also made buckets, barrels and stools. It may well have been the job of the older children to set out the stall at the front of the house and try to sell the family wares.

A blacksmith or 'smithy.' Iron was a very important material to the Anglo-Saxons. Blacksmiths used iron to make everything from fish-hooks to swords.

Families in Jorvik were not poor. We know that a family's diet was varied – people ate plenty of fish such as herring, eels, shellfish and fresh water fish. They also ate chicken, geese, duck, guillemot (a diving sea bird) and cranes, as well as fruit, nuts and seeds. People could also afford luxury goods – pottery wine containers from Germany and a woman's silk cap from the Middle East have been found.

An original cup and bowl made in Coppergate, with modern copies on the right.

18

There seems to have been a big demand for amber jewellery. The stone was probably imported from Denmark.

CHURCHES

After AD 597, **missionaries** encouraged the **pagan** Anglo-Saxons to become Christian. This meant that more parish churches were built in towns. In eleventh-century Norwich there were forty-six. By the late Anglo-Saxon period we see another aspect of family life – the act of worship in the local church. Look below at the Anglo-Saxon church of St. Martin's in Wareham. It was built by the north gate of the town. This was very common in the burghs. Travellers could pray for a safe journey and leave a gift of money at the church. Also, the church tower was used as a look-out for Viking attacks.

We now have a picture of late Anglo-Saxon England as a well-organized and prosperous country. Perhaps it is not surprising that two powerful leaders tried to conquer it in 1066!

The church of St. Martin's, Wareham. This attractive church is typical of the large numbers of churches built in the tenth and eleventh centuries.

MEN, WOMEN AND CHILDREN

The status of an Anglo-Saxon man depended on the amount of land he owned. The royal families controlled many large estates of land. Below royalty, were the **nobles** of varying wealth. They were given land if they supported the king. Nobles had to provide **warriors** in time of war, repair the king's defences and build bridges on his land. Below the nobility were freemen who either owned or rented smaller plots of land. Beneath the freemen were the slaves who carried out a lot of the heavy, dirty work on the **estates**. This quote from the writer Alcuin shows the difference between rich and poor:

'Rich people have many clothes, while others [poor people] persist with cold. Some gorge on feasts. Others die of hunger. The wealth of the rich is the hunger of the poor.'

This is a scene from Frank's casket (around 720 AD). This is Wayland the Smith's brother Egil, defending his home against warriors.

Military skills and fighting were important to the Anglo-Saxon man. He was expected to defend the family home or fight for his lord or king when required. If you look carefully at the carving of the man defending his home, you will see some of the weapons of Anglo-Saxon warfare. The wealthiest warriors wore shirts of chain mail and helmets. A chain-mail shirt has been discovered in York.

WELL-TO-DO WOMEN

We know a lot about the lives of well-to-do Anglo-Saxon women. We know that women could own property. Marriage also made them better-off. When they got married they received 'morgengifu' – or the 'morning gift'. It was a large sum of money or land given directly to a married woman. If a woman did not like her husband she could leave him. If she took her children with her, she was allowed to keep half of the family property.

After the Saxon period women did not have these rights again until the twentieth century. Records show that many powerful women owned great amounts of wealth.

This helmet belonged to an Anglo-Saxon man named Oshere.

Women wore gold headbands like these. This shows us how wealthy some Anglo-Saxon women were.

One woman, Eadgifu the Fair, owned more than 27,000 acres of land. Another, Aeolflaed, 'Lady of the Mercians,' was Alfred the Great's daughter. When her husband became ill, she began ruling Mercia and carried on after his death. In the early tenth century she founded many burghs and commanded armies to fight against the Welsh and the Vikings.

Most married women worked very hard at running the household. We believe their status here was very high too. Women wore strange, key-shaped objects around their waists. These are known as 'girdle-hangers' or mock-keys, and they seemed to be a sign that the women ran the household and held all the keys to the important chests and boxes.

(Below) Women spinning and weaving. Good-quality cloth was very expensive. This illustration is from an eleventh-century manuscript.

(Above) A silk cap from the Middle East – A luxury piece of clothing.

WORKING WOMEN

We can also learn about women's work from names. The ending 'ster' in Anglo-Saxon means 'woman's job'. The word 'spinster' today means 'unmarried' but in Anglo-Saxon meant 'spinner'. This was, along with weaving – 'webster' – a highly skilled and important job. Other examples are 'baxter' – baker, 'tapster' – server, and 'brewster'– brewer.

Ploughman and boy. Working in the fields must have been cold and miserable for a young boy, despite his cloak.

CHILDREN

Most children did not go to school. They were taught important skills by their family – fighting and farming for boys and baking, spinning, weaving and embroidery for girls. Poor children probably had to help out in the fields. Life must have been hard. One ploughman is recorded as saying:

'I have a boy to urge on the oxen with a stick; now he is hoarse because of the cold weather and all his shouting'.

23

CLOTHES

We know about how the early Anglo-Saxons dressed from objects found in the many cemeteries that have been **excavated**. In pre-Christian (pagan) times, when wealthy people died they were buried fully clothed, with their valued possessions.

WOMEN

From the brooches that have been found it is clear that early Saxons liked colour and ornament. Amongst some women, the 'peplos', a tubular woollen dress was fastened by two brooches to strings of beads around the neck. Sometimes a central brooch was worn on the chest to fasten the 'peplos' to an undergarment. Other women were similarly dressed, except the undergarment had long sleeves fastened by wrist clasps. By the later period, the 'peplos' dress was replaced by a fuller, ankle-length tunic, worn over a close-fitting undergarment. The tunic was belted at the waist and many pictures show women with their heads covered with head-dresses. Less jewellery was worn.

This is a model of a female pagan burial found in Surrey. Notice the 'peplos' dress and the jewellery on the wrist.

MEN

We think men wore a linen shirt as an undergarment with a short tunic – a 'crytel' – worn to the upper thigh on top. This would have been belted at the waist and worn with a cloak, perhaps a short one if the wearer was working in the fields.

(Above) The world's most famous sock, made with a special needle style imported from Scandinavia.

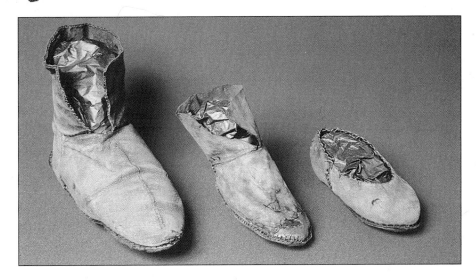

In the Anglo-Saxon period, the 'crytels' became longer and fuller and were worn with rectangular cloaks fastened by a brooch. The fashionable, reasonably wealthy man wore a leather pouch and a knife – a **scramasax** – on his belt.

Slip-on boots and shoes. These were cut and sewn on a wooden 'last' a model of a human foot.

Overgarments, possibly made from animal skins, would be worn in the long, cold winters. Britain was cold and wet, so footwear was important. We know that in Jorvik, high-quality knitted socks kept feet warm as did the crafted leather boots and shoes. Throughout the period, bone and antler combs were used for brushing hair.

Judging by the many bone combs found all over England, Anglo-Saxons took a lot of trouble over their hair. But lice and fleas would have been a constant problem!

HEALTH AND SANITATION

We have recently learned a lot more about health and living conditions in Anglo-Saxon times. Archaeologists have looked at skeletons and remains in sewage and rubbish pits in Coppergate.

ILLNESS AND DEATH

Most people did not live to the age of thirty. They suffered badly from a condition called osteoarthritis. This is a disease in which joints such as the knees, hips and bones in the back become stiff and painful. This was caused by doing a lot of heavy field work – lifting and carrying – in a damp climate.

A large number of women died in their early twenties, during childbirth. A Norwich churchyard contained a large number of baby burials, which points to poor living conditions and a high infant death rate. Skeletons can tell us about the problems of everyday life – broken limbs, sword cuts, tooth abscesses and bone infections. Life was certainly very uncomfortable.

This skeleton was excavated at an Anglo-Saxon cemetery in East Sussex. Bodies, whether buried or cremated, were often placed under mounds, or sometimes wooden structures.

RUBBISH AND SEWAGE PITS

The remains of 1,000-year-old rubbish and sewage pits were analysed. The results showed that most people would have had **parasites** in their intestines – usually whipworm and maw worm. Anglo-Saxons would have suffered from indigestion, diarrhoea and terrible stomach cramps. The poisonous corncockle weed found its way into bread and porridge and would have caused dreadful bouts of stomach ache. With so much waste lying around, flies, beetles and lice spread quickly. Cesspits were often dug next to wells, so the water would never have been clean. Children played in this rotting mess, where rats lived. By our standards the conditions in Jorvik and all Anglo-Saxon towns were filthy!

When analysed this 1,000-year-old human excrement was full of parasite eggs.

A late Anglo-Saxon toilet. You can see the seat at the bottom of the pit. Toilets were usually dug behind houses and could have easily overflowed with rain-water. They were also dangerously close to the wells.

LEISURE

Life for ordinary people during the Anglo-Saxon period was very hard. But we do know it wasn't all work and no play and there were a number of pastimes that people enjoyed.

RICH AND ROYAL FAMILIES

Rich and royal families enjoyed hunting. It was a great occasion that would have ended with huge feasts in the great halls. For larger game such as deer or boar, specially-trained dogs were used, controlled with hunting horns. For smaller game such as hare or birds, falcons would be used. Falcons were high-status animals and the mark of a very rich person. If an ordinary person hunted, it was usually to feed his family.

Hunting. Only very wealthy men could afford to hunt in this way. Good horses were very expensive.

A Viking board game. The jet pieces have been put on a modern board. It appears to be a cross between chess and draughts.

28

POORER PEOPLE

Despite the long working day, recent finds tell us that there was time for leisure in poorer families. At Jorvik, board games were played with carved jet pieces. Ivory dice may have been used with these games or separately for gambling. Music was played – a set of pan-pipes has been found, carved from a single block of wood. The pan-pipes could produce a five-note scale. We can only guess as to how widespread these pastimes were over the whole of Anglo-Saxon England.

A winter pastime was skating. Archaeologists have found a number of bone skates shaped from foot bones of horses and cows. This suggests that winters were very cold and that rivers froze over. Skates would have provided a speedy means of transport and it is highly likely that races and games would have been organized.

Thanks to these discoveries and others such as Sutton Hoo, archaeologists have been able to create a very clear picture of what life was like in Saxon Britain. We can now imagine how a Saxon family would have lived.

Pan-pipes. You can imagine music drifting down the alley-ways and narrow streets of Jorvik.

A skate. The lower surfaces were polished to increase the speed of the skates.

GLOSSARY

Bede An eighth-century monk and historian who wrote the *History of the English Church and People.*

Beowulf A long, exciting Anglo-Saxon poem about warriors, monsters and dragons.

Cauldron A large cooking-pot, usually with handles.

Commerce Trade. The buying and selling of goods.

Communal Something that can be used by everyone in a community.

Cultivate To sow, grow and harvest crops.

Culture The way of life and beliefs of a particular group of people.

Danelaw The area granted to Viking settlers in the late ninth century. It was the land to the east of a line from Chester to London.

Estates Large areas of agricultural land owned by one powerful person.

Excavated Dug up from the ground.

Fertile Having enough nutrients to allow plants to grow strong and healthy.

Kinship A close-knit group of blood relatives.

Missionaries The people who try and convert, or change people into believing in their religion.

Nobles A high ranking, property-owning group, with special privileges.

Pagan A person who does not believe in a religion.

Parasites Organisms that live in the intestines and feed off food in them.

Roman Empire A huge area of Europe, Asia and North Africa which was under Roman rule from 395 AD to 476 AD.

Scramasax A small knife worn by men.

Smithies Blacksmiths. They made everyday iron objects by heating up the iron until it was soft, and moulding it into the right shape.

Subsistence Producing just the right amount of food to survive on.

Threshing Hitting ears of wheat with sticks to separate the grain.

Thatch Straw or weeds which are woven together to make a roof.

Timber-post houses Houses supported on all sides by wooden posts.

Turf A piece of grass cut just below the surface of the soil, used as fuel.

Vikings Raiders from Norway and Denmark who settled in Britain from the eighth to the eleventh centuries.

Warriors Specially trained fighters or soldiers.

Wattle and daub Intertwined branches smeared with mud and animal dung and used to make walls.

Wood turning A method of shaping wooden objects. The wood is turned by a leather thong and shaped by a sharp metal tool.

BOOKS TO READ

For younger readers:

Place, Robin, *Saxon Villages* (Wayland, 1989)

Triggs, Tony, *Saxon Invaders and Settlers* (Wayland, 1992)

Triggs, Tony, *The Saxons* (Oliver and Boyd, 1982)

Wood, Tim, *The Saxons and the Normans* (Ladybird, 1989)

For older readers:

Ellersby, Jean, *The Anglo-Saxon Household* (Cambridge University Press, 1986)

Middleton, Hadyn, *Living in the Past – The Dark Ages* (Blackwell, 1984)

Lloyd, Jean, *Children of Stow* (Micro Press) An excellent reconstruction of the life of West Stow. Available from the visitors' centre at West Stow Anglo-Saxon village.

PLACES TO VISIT

The British Museum, London.
You can see the superb treasure of Sutton Hoo, in its own room.

The Jorvik Centre, York.
Travel back in time to an important city during the late Anglo-Saxon period.

Offa's Dyke, Shropshire and Gloucestershire.
A long ditch and bank built as a defence against the Welsh. Can be viewed west of Mainstone, Shropshire and at Baker's Hill, Gloucestershire.

Southampton City Museum.
Contains many of the finds of Hamwic.

Wallington, Oxfordshire.
One of Alfred's burghs which has the original line of the ramparts and some of the street patterns still visible.

Wareham, Dorset.
You can still walk around the town on the original Anglo-Saxon walls made of turf.

West Stow, near Bury St Edmonds, Suffolk.
Superbly reconstructed early Anglo-Saxon village with a visitors' centre.

There are also many excellent examples of Anglo-Saxon churches around the country.

INDEX

Figures in **bold** are illustrations. Glossary entries are shown by the letter g.